STRANGE HISTORIES
THE GREEKS

Fiona Macdonald

Chrysalis Children's Books

◀ Ancient Greek women dancing, gossiping, playing music and sitting quietly at home.

First published in the UK in 2003 by
Chrysalis Children's Books
An imprint of Chrysalis Books Group Plc
The Chrysalis Building, Bramley Road,
London W10 6SP

Paperback edition first published in 2005

Produced by
Monkey Puzzle Media Ltd
Gissing's Farm, Fressingfield
Suffolk IP21 5SH, UK

Designer: Jamie Asher
Editor: Kate Phelps
Picture Research: Lynda Lines

ISBN 1 84138 665 0 (hb)
ISBN 1 84458 253 1 (pb)

British Library Cataloguing in Publication Data for this book
is available from the British Library.

Printed in China
10 9 8 7 6 5 4 3 2 1

Acknowledgements
We wish to thank the following individuals and
organizations for their help and assistance and for
supplying material in their collections: AKG 2 (Peter
Connolly), 3 (Peter Connolly), 8 (Peter Connolly), 9 top
(Erich Lessing), 11 top (Erich Lessing), 11 bottom (Araldo
de Luca), 14 bottom (Erich Lessing), 17 top (Peter
Connolly), 18 top (Pirozzi), 20 top (Peter Connolly), 22
(Erich Lessing), 24 both (Erich Lessing), 28 (Erich
Lessing), 29 (Erich Lessing); Ancient Art and Architecture
Collection 6 both (R Sheridan), 9 bottom (R Sheridan), 14
top (R Sheridan), 21 bottom (R Sheridan); Art Archive 27
bottom (National Archaeological Museum, Athens/Dagli
Orti); Bildarchiv Preussicher
Kulturbestitz/Antikenmuseum, Berlin) 12 bottom; British
Museum, London 10; C M Dixon front cover and back
cover left, 1, 4 bottom, 7, 12 top, 13, 17 bottom, 19, 23 top,
25; Corbis 18 bottom (Dave G Houser), 31 (Gianni Dagli
Orti); Corbis Digital Stock back cover right, 5; Digital Vision
26; Mary Evans Picture Library 27 top; Topham Picturepoint
15, 16 top, 21 top, 23 bottom. Artwork by Michael Posen.

LOOK FOR THE STATUE

Look for the statue in boxes like this. Here you will
find extra facts, stories and other interesting
information about the strange world of the Greeks.

CONTENTS

▶ *Ancient Greek men fighting, dancing, making sacrifices to the gods, and setting off on a journey.*

MEET THE GREEKS

The Greeks were the most powerful people in Europe from around 600–200 BC.

They were not just powerful but also very proud of their cities, their soldiers, their arts and crafts, their poems and plays, their thinkers, their scientists and their politicians. They pitied people who were not Greeks and who did not enjoy their civilized Greek way of life.

Greece was divided into many city-states, which were cities with farms and countryside around them. All city-states were fierce rivals, and their citizens loved to call each other names. Athenians were 'smug and bossy', Spartans were 'cheats and liars', Corinthians were 'soft', and Thebans were 'traitors', which was the worst insult of all.

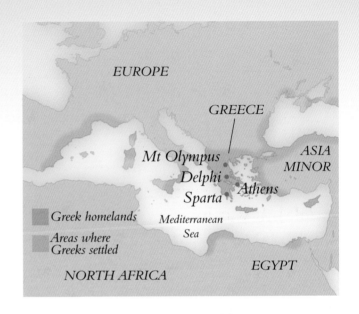

EUROPE

GREECE

Mt Olympus
Delphi
Sparta
Athens

ASIA MINOR

Greek homelands

Areas where Greeks settled

Mediterranean Sea

NORTH AFRICA

EGYPT

▲ *The ancient Greek homelands. The area shaded in red shows where Greek people lived. Greek families also migrated to settle in colonies all round the Mediterranean Sea, in North Africa, Italy, Sicily and France.*

▶ *This gold death-mask is thought to portray Agamemnon, one of the earliest Greek kings, who ruled the city-state of Mycenae around 1500 BC.*

4

Each city-state had its own laws. Some of these were very old. Citizens claimed that they had been made by gods or by mythical kings who probably never existed. (This is not as strange as it sounds; it was a way of saying that the old laws deserved respect.) Other laws were new and led to new fashions in government. The most important of these was democracy (government by the people). It was invented in Athens around 500 BC. However, only male citizens over 30 could take part. Women, foreigners, young men and slaves were banned.

▼ *The Parthenon (temple of the goddess Athena) stood at the heart of Athens, the most powerful city-state in Greece.*

SPEAK LIKE A GREEK

The ancient Greeks thought their language was the best in the world. They called foreigners 'barbarians', because their words sounded like silly sheep bleating, 'baa, baa, baa'.

Hello/goodbye: ***khaire*** (say 'khy-re')
Please: **ei soi dokei** (say 'ay soy dok-ay')
Thank you: **kharin oida soi** (say 'khar-in oy-da soy')
Yes: **nai** (say 'ny')
No: **oukhi** (say 'ook-hi')
Where?: **pou** (say 'poo')
When?: **pote** (say 'po-tay')
Help!: **boethei** (say 'bo-air-thay')

MAKING A LIVING

Greece was not a comfortable environment. The Greek landscape was wild and mountainous. The Greek climate was harsh, with scorching summers and stormy winters. Worst of all, Greece lay in a violent earthquake zone. Travel overland was very difficult. It was often easier to go by sea, though shipwrecks were common. So were pirate attacks.

But the Greeks were great survivors. Most people lived in the country and worked on farms. To grow crops, Greek farmers built terraces, like steps in steep, rocky hillsides, and dug ditches to carry water from mountain streams.

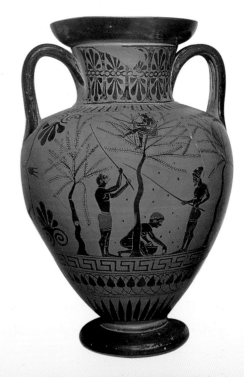

▲ *This vase shows a Greek boy, armed with a stick, climbing high into the branches of an olive tree to harvest the ripe fruit (see box, right).*

▼ *The Pleistos Gorge (rocky valley) near Delphi, in southern Greece shows the wild, rocky landscape in which the Greeks lived.*

WHY DID GREEK FARMERS HIT THEIR TREES?

Each year, farmers gathered ripe olives by beating the trees until the fruit fell down. Then they crushed the olives between stones to get oil. This was eaten raw in food, used for cooking, as a skin cleanser and hair conditioner, as a medicine, to soften leather, for burning in lamps, as a prize in sports competitions and as an offering to the gods.

Farmers' main crops were barley, grapes and olives. They also grew onions, lettuces and garlic and kept pigs, scraggy sheep and goats. They went hunting for hares, deer and even hedgehogs, if no other meat could be found. Their wives and children gathered mushrooms, wild fruit and nuts in the forests, hoping not to meet wild boars or bears.

Farm produce had to last all through the winter. There were no freezers or refrigerators. Cheese was wrapped in leaves or floated in jars of oil. Barley was ground between stones, mixed with oil, seeds and spices, covered with bran and stored in wooden tubs. (Weeks later, this sticky paste was eaten raw. Even the Greeks did not really like it.)

▼ *This terracotta (baked clay) statue shows a Greek man sawing wood. Greek farmers usually built their own homes, and made their own furniture and farm tools. But there were also skilled craftworkers living in Greek cities. They made pottery, jewellery and fine furniture for rich citizens to buy.*

THE GREEKS AT HOME

Greek houses changed size, as the families inside them grew. Most ordinary homes began with just a living room and a bedroom, but over the years, homeowners added more rooms. All this building work made Greek streets messy and confusing.

Rich families also built new rooms, to display their wealth. They added luxuries such as running water, from diverted streams. But, because there were no drains, they still used buckets for lavatories like everyone else. They hung woven rugs on the walls and bought carved wooden furniture, including couches, chests, chairs and low tables.

DANGEROUS AFTER DARK

At night, Greek city streets could be dangerous. You might meet prowling robbers, muggers and hooligans, drunken partygoers or even enemy spies. Or you might trip over people sleeping rough in doorways, or slip and fall on the rough ground. People who needed to go out at night took an escort of slaves with flaming torches and big sticks.

► *This reconstruction drawing is based on the remains of a real Greek house, built in Athens around 450 BC. Only wealthy families could afford a big house like this; ordinary people's homes were much smaller, less strongly-built, and often much less tidy.*

Many Greek men, and all Greek women, worked at home. These women are spinning wool into thread (left) and winding it on to a wooden frame (right). Women were expected to spin and weave for several hours every day. It was their job to make all the clothes, rugs and blankets that their families needed.

Greek families worried about security. There was only one door into a house, and it was guarded by a slave or a dog. Walls (made of mud brick) had to be strong enough to stop 'wall-diggers' (burglars) breaking in at night. Privacy was also important. Most houses had a room for women only that men could not enter. They had a separate room of their own for entertaining male friends.

Houses could sometimes seem like prisons. Women, children and slaves all needed a man's permission to leave. Slaves and women from poor families were allowed out to fetch water or buy food. But rich women, from 'respectable' families, could only leave to take part in religious ceremonies and funerals or to visit other women. To stop anyone seeing them, they had to cover their faces with veils.

Hestia (below) was the goddess who guarded Greek homes. The hearth-fire in each house was sacred to her. It was very bad luck if it ever went out.

FAMILY LIFE

The Greeks did not have a word for 'family'. They had 'clans' and 'households' instead. A 'clan' meant people descended from one ancestor. A 'household' meant people living together, and might include a married couple, their children, grandparents, servants and slaves.

Greek marriages were often arranged. Brides had no chance to choose a partner or say 'no'. Husbands and wives may never have met before their wedding day. Once married, they were not equal. Husbands had almost total power over money and legal matters, though wives were in charge of running the home.

NO RIGHTS FOR WOMEN

In ancient Greece, most women could not:
- vote
- serve on juries
- be doctors, lawyers or teachers
- take part in government
- run big businesses
- own houses and land
- ask for a divorce
- leave their house alone
- talk to men except their close family or slaves

◄ *A mother (left) helps her daughter (right) dress for her wedding. Before leaving their parents' home to live with their new husbands, Greek girls cut off some or all of their hair, and offered it to the goddess Artemis. Then they veiled their faces, and were carried at night in a torchlight procession to their groom's family home, where they would spend the rest of their married lives.*

Parents, grandparents and children sharing a family meal. Greek households were often large, so poor peoples' small homes were cramped and crowded. To escape, men and boys spent much of their time outside.

The Greeks were fond of children. But babies born to Greek families did not always survive. Their father had the power to decide their fate. He might not want too many boys, since family land would have to be split between them when he died. And girls had to take money to their husband's family when they married. Unwanted babies were abandoned or given to childless couples.

If a father chose to keep a baby, it was welcomed with special rituals. Slaves pinned strands of wool (for a girl) or olive twigs (for a boy) to the street door to announce the birth. Then, seven days later, the baby's father picked it up and ran round the hearth with no clothes on! The rest of the household sang hymns. Three days after that, the baby was given a name.

▶ This Greek statue of a mother and child was made around 300 BC. A wife's main task was to produce a son. If she failed to do this, her husband might divorce her. Greek doctors also thought that having children was good for women's health, even though many Greek women died in childbirth.

GROWING UP

Only one Greek child in ten learned how to read and write because most did not go to school. Girls stayed at home and learned useful skills like weaving and cooking from their mothers or from slaves. Boys from poor families had to work and earn money.

If boys did go to school, they were taken there by a slave. He stayed with them during lessons and made sure they paid attention. Boys studied reading, writing, maths and lots of poetry (adults hoped this would teach them to be brave like the heroes in the poems). They used an abacus to do sums or worked out the answers in their heads. The Greeks had no signs for numbers, so written sums were impossible.

▲ Greek parents made their children work hard, but they loved them, too. This tombstone is carved with a touching portrait of a girl who died young, and her pet dog.

◀ A Greek schoolboy (centre) stands in front of his teacher (left), who is holding a scroll with writing on it. (The Greeks did not have books.) The boy's slave sits on the right. He holds a big stick, to punish the boy if he does not learn his lessons well.

Greek children loved to play, and many of their games and toys were like ours today. They had dolls, rattles, yo-yos, dice, spinning tops, seesaws and puppets, and they played hockey, tug-of-war and blind man's buff. But some of their games were rather different. One favourite was played with the anklebones of dead sheep.

Teenagers were kept busy, so they would not misbehave. Girls were married at 12 or 14. Teenage boys were made to work or study, or they were sent to sports centres to get healthy exercise. At 18, they had to join the army for two years.

GROWING UP IN SPARTA

In Sparta, a Greek city-state, boys' lives were very hard. At seven, they were taken away from their families to live in army camps. They were kept cold and hungry, and baths were banned. They were often beaten. If they died, it proved they were too weak to survive. Spartan girls stayed at home but learned tough sports and fighting like boys.

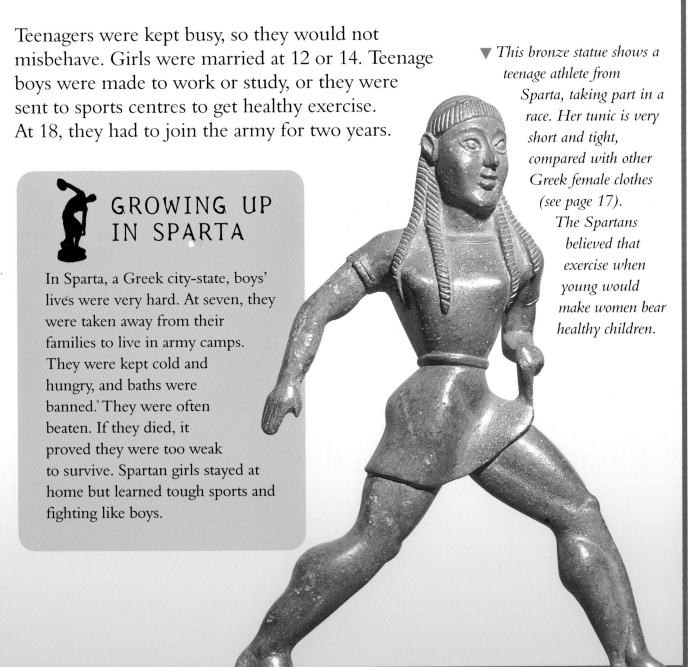

▼ This bronze statue shows a teenage athlete from Sparta, taking part in a race. Her tunic is very short and tight, compared with other Greek female clothes (see page 17). The Spartans believed that exercise when young would make women bear healthy children.

FOOD AND DRINK

Greek food was plain and simple. A typical meal might be bread, salt fish, fruit or vegetables and olive oil. The usual drink, even at breakfast time, was wine mixed with water. Some foreigners said Greek food was boring, but the Greeks despised fancy foods, such as rich sauces.

Meat was an expensive luxury. Many families looked forward to religious festival days because that was their only chance to eat it. Priests roasted animals that had been sacrificed to the gods over fires in front of temples and handed out slices of meat to worshippers. The Greeks also shared another favourite food – barley cakes sweetened with honey – with their gods. Sugar was unknown in ancient Greek times.

▲ *Preparing for a Greek feast. This terracotta statue shows a female servant grilling pieces of meat over an open fire.*

◄ *Men relaxing and drinking wine during a symposium (male dinner party). The Greeks always drank wine mixed with water.*

DID ALL GREEK FOOD TASTE GOOD?

The ancient Greeks ate foods that some people might not like today, such as goats' lungs (the air inside whistled as they were cooked), sea urchins (raw and still alive) and octopus (very tough and chewy). When food was scarce, in wartime or drought years, Greeks ate almost anything they could find, including iris roots, beechnuts, lupin seeds and grasshoppers.

The Greeks liked cheese but made it from sheep's milk, not cow's. They thought cow's milk was unhealthy. They also enjoyed soups made with lentils and chickpeas. But many Greek people would not eat beans. They believed one philosopher (called Pythagoras) who claimed that beans contained the souls of the dead.

Normally, Greeks ate sitting on low chairs. But on special occasions, such as men-only dinner parties, they ate lying down. Diners relaxed on long, low couches, which had room for two, side by side. This was so comfortable that they often dozed off between courses. Or maybe the wine was to blame?

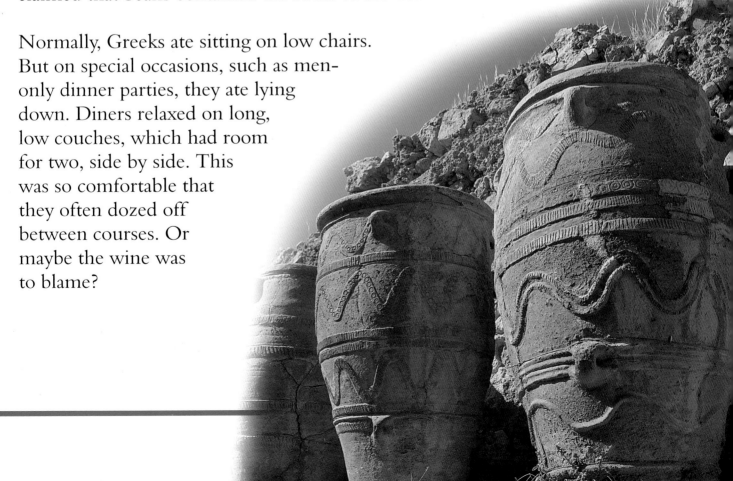

▼ *The Greeks used pottery jars to store wine, grain and oil. When splashed outside with water, they kept the contents cool. Because they were made of clay, mice and rats could not chew their way inside. These massive jars, made on the Greek island of Crete, hold hundreds of litres each.*

LOOKING GOOD

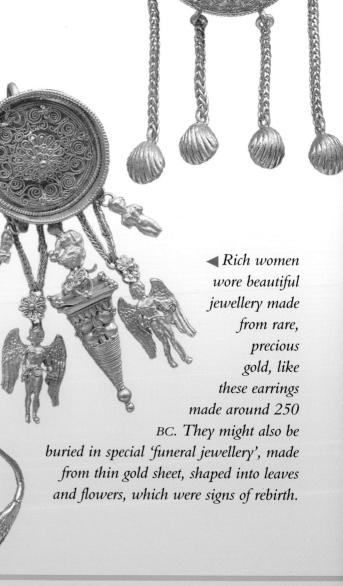

Clothes for Greek men, women and children were all made from a single piece of cloth wrapped round the body and held in place by pins. Underneath, some men wore a loincloth, and some women covered their chest with a soft cloth band. But most Greeks wore no underwear at all!

Clothes for men and children were usually knee-length. Women's clothes reached the floor, and so did robes for priests and kings. Most cloth was woven at home, from sheep's wool, by wives, mothers and female slaves.

Fancy cloth woven from Chinese silk and dyed purple with 'murex' (rotted shellfish) was worn by rich, powerful people. It could be bought at markets for a high price. But some scholars deliberately wore old, shabby clothes as a sign that they were thinking of more important things. One famous philosopher, Diogenes (about 400–325 BC), gave up clothes altogether and lived in a big pottery jar.

◄ *Rich women wore beautiful jewellery made from rare, precious gold, like these earrings made around 250 BC. They might also be buried in special 'funeral jewellery', made from thin gold sheet, shaped into leaves and flowers, which were signs of rebirth.*

16

Greek women painted their faces with make-up and used hair dye and perfume. They let their hair grow long and tied it back with ribbons or jewelled headbands. Men had short hair and neatly trimmed beards. Slaves had their hair cut very short to show they were not free.

▶ *As you can see from these copies of vase-paintings, clothes for Greek men, women and children were all the same basic shape – a loose tube!*

▼ *Greek women (and men!) liked to wear perfume and scented body powder. A few men used make-up and hair-dye, too. This perfume-flask, made around 500 BC, is shaped like the head of a helmeted soldier.*

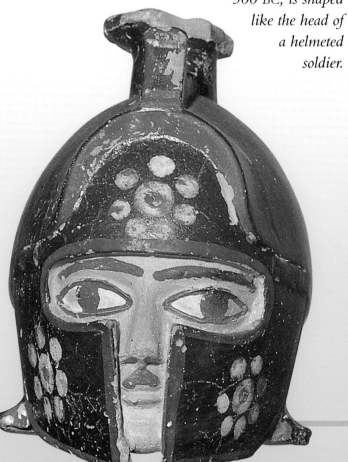

MAN-SIZED MEASUREMENTS

The ancient Greeks measured length and distance in units based on an average-sized adult man.

1 finger = almost 2 cm
4 fingers = 1 palm = 7.5 cm
12 fingers = 1 hand-span = 22.5 cm
16 fingers = 1 foot = 30 cm
24 fingers = 1 cubit = 46 cm
2.5 feet = 1 pace = 75 cm
6 feet = 1 stretch (both arms) = 1.8m
600 feet = 1 stadion = 178m

FUN AND GAMES

The Greeks took life very seriously. They loved to discuss important questions, such as 'When did the world begin'. They paid for some of the world's best scientists and cleverest thinkers to come and live in their city-states. But they also enjoyed parties, singing, dancing, going to the theatre, telling stories, laughing at jokes and playing games.

Professional storytellers, called 'song-stitchers', performed in streets and markets and at festivals. They often added their own extra details to bring the stories up to date. Guests at dinner parties also told jokes and stories, and played silly games like kottabos, which involved flicking drops of wine at a target.

◀ This is a Roman copy of one of the most famous Greek statues ever made. (Sadly, the original has disappeared.) It shows an athlete throwing a discus - a favourite Olympic sport.

◀ This picture shows a Greek amphitheatre where plays were performed. The first Greek plays were religious. They retold myths about the gods. But they soon developed into great entertainment that lasted all day long. The audience was mostly men. Greeks believed that tragic plays were too sad for women to watch, and comic plays were too rude.

The Greeks liked music and dancing because they were fun. They were also part of many religious ceremonies. Sometimes, worshippers got carried away by the beat. Stories were told of *maenads*, wild women who left their homes and ran to the mountains, where they tore wild beasts limb from limb.

Sport was the most important entertainment of all. The famous Olympic Games, held in honour of the god Zeus, was just one of many sports festivals open to all Greek athletes. Like football and baseball today, they inspired fierce rivalry and local pride. Champions were sponsored by rich businessmen and were rewarded with free food for life by their home city. Winning athletes wore crowns of laurel leaves, pine branches or wild celery.

FIRST CATCH YOUR TORTOISE

One favourite musical instrument was the lyre. Lyres were used to play solemn, gentle music but they hid a bloodthirsty secret. They had a U-shaped frame, seven strings and a sound box (which increased the volume). At first, their sound boxes were made from tortoiseshells, their frames from cattle horns and their strings from animal gut. Later, lyres were mostly made of wood.

▼ *Chariot racing at the Olympics. A charioteer drives a team of four horses (count the legs!) twelve times round a track 1100m long. Chariots often crashed and overturned, and drivers died. The winner was the owner of the chariot and horses, not the charioteer who took part in the race.*

SUPERHUMAN

Greek gods and goddesses were like humans but bigger and better. They were taller, stronger and more beautiful. They had magic powers and lived forever. Many gods helped their favourite people or cities. But they could also be mischievous, fierce and cruel.

▶ *This is a modern reconstruction of the statue of the mighty goddess Athena that stood in the Parthenon temple in Athens (see page 5). The original was made of gold and ivory, and was about 10m high.*

To keep the gods happy, the Greeks gave them presents, called sacrifices. At first, these were real people. Young girls were the usual sacrifice when an army set off for war. Later, the Greeks gave animals, food or wine.

The Greeks built huge temples but they didn't go inside. A temple was a god's house and too holy, except for priests and priestesses. A few gods and goddesses were worshipped secretly, in the wild countryside or in hidden caves. Some special underground rituals to honour Demeter, goddess of fertility, were so mysterious that no one knows what went on, even today. Anyone who tried to tell was killed instantly.

A-Z OF GODS AND GODDESSES

This 'family' of gods and goddesses lived on Olympus, the highest mountain in Greece.

Aphrodite – goddess of love and beauty
Apollo – god of music and learning
Ares – god of war
Artemis – goddess of young girls and wild creatures
Athena – goddess of wisdom, art and craft, and war
Demeter – goddess of grain and growing crops
Dionysus – god of wine and wildness
Hera – goddess of women and marriage
Hermes – messenger of the gods
Hestia – goddess of hearths and homes
Poseidon – god of earthquakes and the sea
Zeus – god of lightning, king of the gods

A ruined temple at Delphi, one of the holiest places in Greece. Temples were shaped like the first Greek houses. Their stone columns were copies of the tree-trunks that held up the house roofs.

Worshippers taking part in mysterious ceremonies to honour the goddess Demeter. They believed that she had the power to make them happy in the life after death.

Spirits living in fields, streams and trees were also worshipped by the Greeks. They believed that some spirits, called oracles, could see into the future. Priests talked to oracle trees and hung prayers in their branches. They also examined the guts of dead animals for omens. At Delphi, a priestess, drugged with smoke from burning leaves, gave answers to questions. People believed the oracle spoke through her words.

THE GREEKS AT WAR

The Greeks were fierce warriors but they usually fought themselves. Rival city-states quarrelled over land and trade. Great cities were destroyed, and many brave men died. Twice, the Greeks united, more or less, to defeat their great enemies, the Persians. They also fought against the Turkish city of Troy.

Most wars were short. Fighting stopped in late summer because soldiers had to help with harvesting. It stopped in winter, too, because the weather was bad. Only the war-like city of Sparta stayed ready to fight all year round. Unlike other Greeks, Spartan soldiers wore uniforms and marched to army bands. The noise of Spartan flute-players could be deafening. Mothers in Sparta wanted their sons to be brave. Before a battle, they told them, 'come back carrying your shield [that is, fit and victorious] or on it [dead!]'.

◀ Famous hero Alexander the Great (see page 27) fighting against the Persians at the Battle of Issus in 333 BC. Against the odds, he led Greek and Macedonian soldiers to victory against the much larger Persian army.

Greek soldiers' metal armour was tough and strong, but it was also very heavy. Each man's kit could weigh over 30 kg.

THE BEST WAY TO WIN?

The Greeks invented fearsome war machines, such as giant crossbows armed with iron-tipped arrows and huge catapults that hurled lumps of rock at enemy walls. They even made flame-throwers. But many Greek soldiers preferred traditional tactics in war. They destroyed crops and cut down olive trees, so everyone starved. They surrounded cities until food and water ran out or the citizens all died of disease.

All citizens were meant to serve as soldiers, but poor men could not afford to. Each Greek hoplite (infantryman) had to buy his own shield, helmet, breastplate, spear, sword and greaves (shin-guards). If poor men did go to war, they fought with cheap weapons like slingshots and had no protection from enemy attack.

Rich Greek city-states built heavy warships (like the modern reconstruction in the picture) to fight against enemy fleets. They were powered by men rowing, as well as by sails. Each ship was armed with a metal-tipped battering ram at the prow (front), designed to smash holes in enemy ships, and sink them.

SICKNESS, DEATH AND BURIAL

The Greeks used magic, medicine, religious ceremonies and, sometimes, science to try and cure disease. But most of them still died young. The average Greek woman lived until she was 35. A man might live longer, maybe until 50. Many children died before they were five years old.

▲ *Many Greek people believed that sickness was sent by the gods. They slept overnight at healing shrines (above) hoping that Asclepius, the god of healing, or his magic snake, would visit them in a dream, and cure them.*

Greek doctors thought that people had four different liquids flowing through their bodies – red blood, green phlegm, yellow bile and black choler – and that too much of any one caused disease. They tested (and tasted!) samples to diagnose illnesses.

One famous doctor had different ideas. His name was Hippocrates (about 460–370 BC). He studied his patients scientifically and said that illness was caused by an unhealthy lifestyle or an unquiet mind. He also said doctors should be clean, neat, slim, sweet smelling and good-looking! Patients would trust them more that way.

If doctors failed to cure a patient, the dead body had to be buried. Greek funerals took place at dawn and were very noisy occasions. Women wept and wailed, scratched their cheeks and cut their hair. After the body was buried, offerings of food were placed on its tomb for nine days. Then the dishes were broken to stop the ghost coming back for more!

▲ *Many Greek tombstones were decorated with scenes from the dead person's life. Here, a woman called Hegeso, who died in the fourth century BC, is shown with her female slave (left), who is handing her a box of jewellery.*

◄ *The Greek women on this piece of pottery are preparing a corpse for burial, while mourners on either side pray, weep and wail. The Greeks usually raised their hands in the air when praying to the gods, because most of the gods lived high above, in the sky.*

 THREE STAGES OF LIFE

Greek legends describe a terrifying monster called the Sphinx. It lay in wait for travellers and would not let them pass until they had answered this riddle: 'What has four legs, then two, then three?' The answer was 'a human' (a baby crawls on four legs, an adult walks on two legs and an old person walks with a stick). If anyone got the answer wrong, the Sphinx ate them.

Greek Facts

Here is a selection of interesting facts about the strange world of the ancient Greeks.

Men only

Women were banned at the Olympic Games. But one mother was so keen to see her son race that she dressed as a man and hid among the crowd. When she saw her son winning, she shouted out with excitement and gave herself away. She was expelled in disgrace.

Trickster

Athenian ruler Peisistratus (about 600–527 BC) seized power by a clever trick. He rushed into town one day, covered in mud and bruises, claiming to have been attacked. He asked the citizens' assembly to give him a bodyguard, and they agreed. He used this bodyguard to defeat his enemies and take control of the city.

Smelly feet

Priests at the temple of Zeus at Dodona, southern Greece, were known as *selloi*, which means 'with unwashed feet'. No one knows why they were so dirty!

▲ *Greek ideas, discoveries and artistic styles still shape our lives today. Many special buildings, like the White House (above), the home of the US president, are designed to look like ancient Greek structures.*

Marathon man

In ancient Greece, urgent wartime messages were carried by fast runners. The most famous was called Pheidippides. It was said that he ran 42 km from a battlefield at Marathon in 490 BC to tell the Athenians that their army had won. He then dropped dead from exhaustion!

Lucky for some

For the Greeks, right was lucky, left was unlucky. When Greek general Xenophon (about 435–354 BC) was preparing for battle in 401 BC, he heard an eagle screeching on his right-hand side. Priests told him this meant he would win. He did.

THE WORLD'S GREATEST WARRIOR?

Most Greeks thought Alexander the Great (356–323 BC) was the greatest soldier who ever lived. Some said he was a god. Alexander became king of Macedonia (north of Greece) when he was only 20 years old. He murdered his younger brother to make sure he never became king. Then he set off to conquer the world. He won a vast empire, stretching from Greece and Egypt to India and Afghanistan. He wanted more, but his army refused to march farther. He died aged 32 in Iraq.

THE ANCIENT GREEKS VISITED BRITAIN

Explorer Pytheas reached Orkney and Shetland around 350 BC. The Greeks also sailed along the coast of Africa and may have crossed the Equator.

▶ *Archimedes invented a machine to make water flow uphill. It is still used today, and is called the 'Archimedian screw' because it turns round and round like a corkscrew.*

I'VE GOT IT!

Greek mathematician and inventor Archimedes (287–212 BC) was one of the greatest scientists of all time. After he discovered how pulleys and levers work, he boasted 'Give me somewhere to stand, and I will move the Earth!'. He also became famous for making a very important discovery (about mass and gravity) in his bath. He was so excited that he jumped out and ran down the street, shouting 'Eureka!' (I've got it!).

◀ *Greek athletes wrestling. The most violent Greek sport was pankration ('total power'), which was a mixture of boxing and wrestling, with no holds barred, except biting and eye-gouging!*

GREEK WORDS

This glossary explains some of the words used in this book that you might not have seen before.

Abacus
Wooden frame with rows of beads. Used as an early kind of calculator.

Assembly
Meeting of citizens in a city-state.

Beechnuts
Small, brown, bitter, chewy nuts from beech trees.

Citizen
Person living in a city-state who had full rights to take part in government and help make laws.

City-state
City and the surrounding land that it controlled.

Clan
People descended from one ancestor. They had a duty to help one another.

Democracy
Government by the people.

Flame-throwers
Long tubes which shoot jets of flame.

▲ *A hoplite (foot-soldier) in a hurry! Many Greek soldiers decorated their shields with symbols of their city-state. This made it easier to recognise friends or enemies in battle.*

Greaves
Shin-guards. Rather like football shin-pads but made of metal.

Hoplites
Soldiers in heavy armour who fought on foot.

Household
People living in the same home.

Loincloth

Strip of cloth wound round the lower body.

Lupin

Flowering plant. The seeds are poisonous, so do not eat them.

Mythical

From a story; not real.

Omens

Signs of what is to come in the future.

Oracles

Spirits that could see into the future.

Philosopher

A highly educated person. Philosophers were often in charge of respected places of learning.

Sacrifices

Offerings to the gods, to give thanks or ask for help.

Sea urchins

Soft, pulpy creatures that live on the seabed. They are covered by a dome-shaped shell.

Slaves

Men, women and children who were not free but belonged to their owners. They could be bought and sold. Some were treated well, others badly.

▼ *Many Greek myths tell fantastic and funny stories about gods and heroes. Here, the hero Heracles is hiding in a big storage jar from a nine-headed monster dog called Cerberus, that guarded the way into the Underworld.*

GREEK PROJECTS

If you want to find out more about the Greeks, here are some ideas for projects.

MAKE A WATER CLOCK

The ancient Greeks did not have clocks with springs, batteries or electricity. They used water clocks, called *clepsydra*, instead. (These went drip-drop instead of tick-tock!) Here is how to make one. It might be best to try this outside as it could be messy.

You will need:
two plastic containers, both about the same size. (You could use big yoghurt pots or the bottom half of two soft drinks bottles.)
a bendy drinking straw
scissors, plastic bricks or a plastic box, a small piece of plastic food wrap, a small rubber band, water

1. Using scissors, carefully make a small hole in one of the containers, near the bottom. It should be just big enough for the straw to fit in.
2. Trim the straw so it looks like the straw in the diagram.
3. Push one end of the straw into the hole. Cover the other end of the straw with food wrap. Use the elastic band to hold the wrap in place.
4. Stand the container on the bricks or box. Put the other container below it, as shown.
5. Fill the top container with water and carefully remove the food wrap and elastic band.
6. See how long the water takes to run out into the lower container. It will be the same every time.

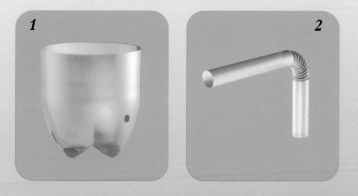

PAINT BACK-TO-FRONT, GREEK-STYLE

Greek craftworkers liked to decorate the pots they made with scenes from everyday life or with pictures of gods and heroes. Often, they used a special back-to-front technique:

1. They drew the outline of the gods or people they wanted to show.
2. They painted the background black, leaving the rest unpainted.
3. Sometimes they added details, like eyes or hair, to the unpainted area.

You will need:

coloured paper, a pen or pencil, black paint, a brush

Follow steps 1 to 3 above and see if you can paint back-to-front in the Greek way.

ENJOY SOME ANCIENT GREEK STORIES

Many stories told by Greek 'song-stitchers' are still popular today. You can find them in your school or public library. Look out for books telling the strange adventures of Greek hero Odysseus and all the magical monsters he met. Or read about brave Greek soldiers and how they conquered their enemies at Troy by a very strange trick.

▲ *This picture from a Greek pot shows the god Zeus marrying the goddess Hera. The spirit of Love (with wings) is placing a crown of flowers on Zeus's head.*

GREEKS ON THE INTERNET

The Internet is a great way to find out more about the Greeks. But the Internet is constantly changing so if you can't find these websites try searching using the word 'Greeks'.

http://www.historyforkids.org/learn/greeks/index.htm

http://www.museum.upenn.edu/Greek_World/Index.html

http://www.upenn.edu/museum/Olympics/olympicintro.html

http://www.perseus.tufts.edu/Olympics

http://www.aesopfables.com/

INDEX